HONEYBEES

INSECTS IN MY BACKYARD

RYAN JAMES

NorwoodHouse Press

Library of Congress Cataloging-in-Publication Data

Names: James, Ryan.
Title: Honeybees / Ryan James.
Description: Buffalo, NY : Norwood House Press, 2025. | Series: Insects in my backyard | Includes glossary and index.
Identifiers: ISBN 9781684502509 (pbk.) | ISBN 9781684502516 (library bound) | ISBN 9781684502523 (ebook)
Subjects: LCSH: Honeybee--Juvenile literature. -
Classification: LCC QL568.A6 J359 2025 | DDC 595.79'9--dc23

Published in 2025 by
Norwood House Press
2544 Clinton Street
Buffalo, NY 14224

Designer: Ocean Books
Editor: Kim Thompson

Photo credits: Cover, p. 1 herain kathatham/Shutterstock.com; p. 5 nikolpetr/Shutterstock.com; p. 6 Cornel Constanin/Shutterstock.com; p. 7 Paulrommer SL/Shutterstock.com; p. 9 Dmytro Khlystun/Shutterstock.com; p. 11 aeiddam0853578919/Shutterstock.com; p. 12 Davide Bonora/Shutterstock.com; p. 13 M.Saidur/Shutterstock.com; p. 15 Kuzmanovic Milos/Shutterstock.com; p. 16 Diga ShumShutterstock.com; p. 17 Lorenzo Bernin/Shutterstock.com; p. 21 inna Reznik/Shutterstock.com

Printed in the United States of America

CPSIA compliance information: Batch #CW25NHP: For further information contact Norwood House Press at 1-800-237-9932.

TABLE OF CONTENTS

WHAT IS A HONEYBEE?

Honeybees are busy **insects** you might find in your backyard. They like to fly around flowers.

BODY PARTS

Honeybees have three body sections. The head is in front. Honeybees have two large black eyes and two **antennae** to help them find flowers.

The thorax is the middle section of a honeybee. It has six legs and two pairs of clear wings.

The abdomen is the back section of a honeybee. It has stripes. It also has a stinger that honeybees use to protect themselves.

TYPES OF HONEYBEES

The western honeybee is golden brown with black stripes. It is found in North America and is the most common honeybee in the United States.

The African honeybee is small and **aggressive**, with dark brown and black coloring. It is found in Africa and some parts of South America.

The Italian honeybee is golden yellow with brown stripes. It is commonly found in Europe, especially in Italy.

The Carniolan honeybee is dark brown with gray stripes. It is found in Slovenia and other countries in Central Europe.

HONEYBEE BEHAVIOR

Honeybees work together to build a **hive**. They use wax from their bodies to fill the hive with honeycomb. The honeycomb's **cells** are used for storing honey and raising young bees.

Honeybees use their long tongues to drink **nectar** from flowers. They use nectar to make honey.

Honeybees do a dance to tell other bees where to find food. This waggle dance shows the direction and distance to the flowers.

WHY ARE HONEYBEES IMPORTANT?

When honeybees visit flowers, they collect **pollen** on their legs. They spread it from flower to flower. This is called pollination. Many plants cannot **reproduce** without pollination.

When honeybees pollinate plants, they support the environment. Pollinated plants can make seeds and fruit. Healthy plants provide food and shelter for many animals.

Honeybees make honey, which people like to eat. Honey is used in some medicines because it has natural healing powers.

GLOSSARY

aggressive (uh-GRES-iv): threatening; ready to attack

antennae (an-TEN-ee): slender, movable, segmented organs on the heads of insects that are used to sense the environment; feelers

cells (selz): small rooms or enclosed spaces; compartments of a honeycomb

hive (hive): a nest for a group of bees

insects (IN-sekts): small animals that have hard outer skeletons instead of backbones and that have three pairs of legs, one or two pairs of wings, and three body sections

nectar (NEK-tur): a sweet liquid produced by flowers

pollen (PAH-luhn): fine yellow powder that is produced in the male parts of flowering plants and that must be spread to female plant parts in order for some plants to reproduce

reproduce (ree-pruh-DOOS): to produce new living things of the same type; to make babies

THINKING QUESTIONS

1. Name a honeybee's three body sections.

2. How are an Italian honeybee and a Carniolan honeybee alike and different?

3. How do honeybees tell others where food can be found?

4. How do the legs of the honeybee help plants?

5. Why are honeybees important?

INDEX

ABOUT THE AUTHOR

Ryan James lives in the western part of North Carolina with his rescue dog Bailey. As a child, he would search for creepy crawlies as he hiked through the forest near his house. When he's not on the hiking or biking trail, he is cheering on his favorite baseball and football teams.